Hi...

c.680 First Saxo...
1094 Building o...
1210 Oldest mis...
c.1145 Nave roofed at triforium height.
1150 Augustinian Canons Regular established.
1290 Clerestory completed and roof raised.
1320 Quire screen carved.
1360 Jesse screen carved.
1370 Two king's bells cast.
1390 Lady Chapel started.
c.1420 Central tower collapses.
1480 West tower added.
1539 Monastic buildings destroyed.
1540 Henry VIII gives church to town.
1662 Grammar school established in St Michael's Loft.

Beginnings

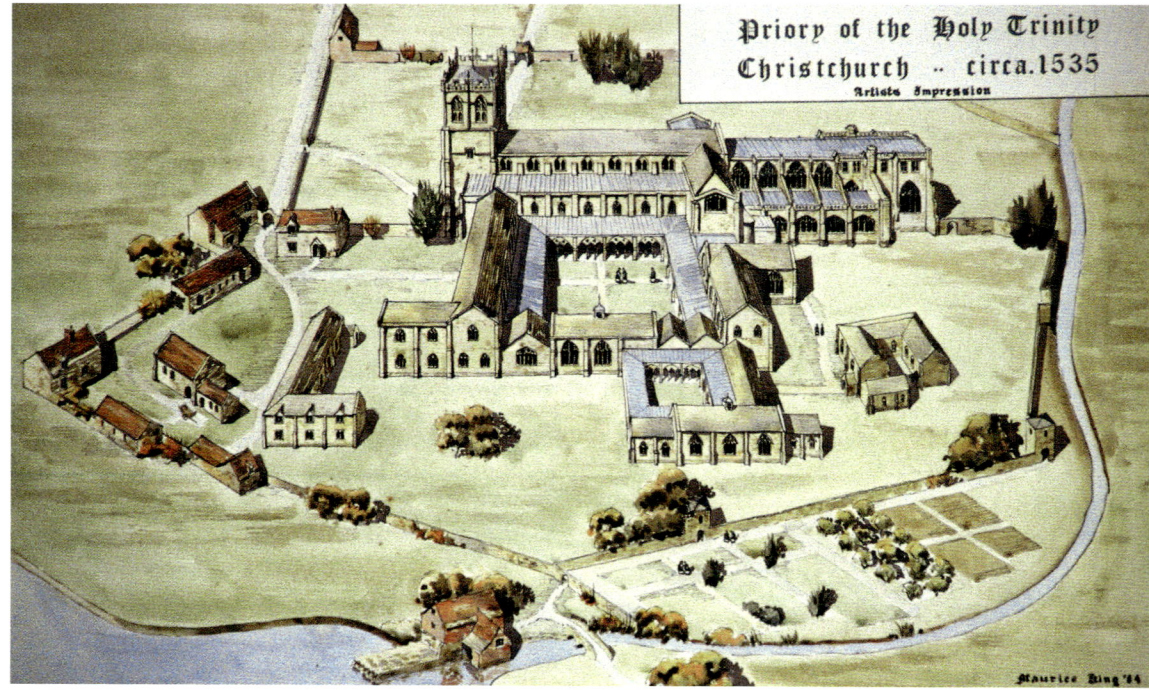

ABOVE: The priory, with conventual buildings as they might have looked in Prior Draper's day just before their destruction by Henry VIII in 1539. From a painting by Maurice King.

Christians have worshipped on this site since the 7th century. Beneath the transepts and great quire of the present church, which was started in 1094 by Ranulf Flambard, later to be Bishop of Durham, lie three crypts from the original Saxon stone church and chapels. Domesday records that in 1086 the Monastery of the Holy Trinity at Toinham (as the fortified Royal Burgh was then called) had 24 secular canons headed by Godric, all of whom not only ministered to the spiritual needs of a wide area but also provided a school, care for the sick, poor and travellers, and owned extensive lands and the mill by the quay.

Flambard's original intention to build his great church on St Catherine's Hill two miles up the Avon valley was 'miraculously' frustrated, so he pulled down the Saxon church and its nine chapels and built over the same site, appropriating the church's revenues to himself. Much of the stone came from the Isle of Wight. Though the master builder may have come from Caen in Normandy, most of the craftsmen would have been local men. By 1150 the main church was complete, cruciform in shape with an apse at the east end, though the central tower and spire were still to be built. Henry of Blois, Bishop of Winchester and King Stephen's brother, with Baldwin de Redvers, Lord of the Manor, persuaded Pope Eugenius III to establish a community of Augustinian Canons Regular, who had to be celibate, to build a complete set of conventual buildings and run the ever-growing work of the monastery. Such was the church's architectural magnificence, with its high altar dedicated to Christ the Saviour, that the town soon became known as Christchurch. For the next 400 years, supported by gifts not only from kings and wealthy patrons, but also countless humble folk, the church grew in a splendour of many architectural styles to produce the magnificent amalgam we see today – the longest parish church in Britain. When in 1539

CHRISTCHURCH PRIORY

A Welcome from the Vicar

We welcome you to our Priory Church. On this site prayer and worship have been offered for over 1,300 years, and in this building for over 900 years, proclaiming Jesus the Son of God, crucified, risen, ascended and glorified Lord of all. As you make your way through this magnificent parish church and admire the remarkable styles of architecture that surround you, remember the countless men and women for whom this place has been a special haven of peace and refuge, a source of spiritual renewal and inspiration. Throughout the centuries, in the great quire the Augustinian monks said their seven Offices of the day and celebrated the Mass. Today we continue that offering in our daily round of prayer and eucharistic worship. There is in this place a real sense of warmth and joy, which I hope you will take with you as you continue your pilgrimage. May God bless you and the places from which you come.

Henry VIII ordered the destruction of the monastic buildings, John Draper, the last prior, successfully petitioned the king to grant the church and churchyard to the townsfolk to be their parish church in perpetuity.

Since Saxon times, for 1,300 years and more, the priests have worked in and through the community here, bringing succour, comfort and guidance to all who seek it, making church and town one in CHRISTCHURCH.

LEFT: *The Miraculous Beam, originally over the nave, but now high above the ambulatory near the Draper Chantry, safe from damage.* ⑭

ABOVE: *An octagonal roundel from a window situated in the new cloister, showing Christ the Carpenter raising the Miraculous Beam.* ⑳

The Miraculous Beam

Legend has it that there was an exceptionally skilled extra carpenter working on the massive roof timbers who was never seen at the pay table or at meals. One day disaster struck. It was discovered that one main beam had been cut a foot too short. The carpenters and masons were all devastated. However, next day the beam was found to be up and in its right place spanning the walls with a foot to spare. There was universal rejoicing, but the extra carpenter could not be found to hear the good news and was never seen again. All agreed that 'He must have been the Christ, the Carpenter of Nazareth', and the high altar was dedicated to Him.

The West End

The west tower, 36.5m (120 ft) high with 176 steps, was built towards the end of the 15th century, replacing the central tower which fell during a storm about 1420. Nearly 10m (33 ft) above the tower shines the famous Christchurch salmon as a weather-vane. Thirteen bells provide an upper and lower peal. Two bells bearing Edward III's head and dated 1370 are named 'St Augustine' and 'All Saints'. They are amongst the oldest regularly rung in England.

The north porch, dating from the early 13th century, is probably the longest in England. Here the prior sat in his huge seat, sheltered from the prevailing south-west wind, to transact business and meet the town's burgesses. The carved stone bosses include the 'Pelican in her Piety', frequently depicted by early Christian sculptors.

The west window, installed in 1861, is known as the *Te Deum* window, and depicts the Matins hymn 'We praise thee, oh God'.

The font is a 20th-century copy of the 1220 marble font which now stands next to the Salisbury Chantry. Part of a Saxon font can be

BELOW: *The carved stone cross at the north end of the north porch roof.* ①

LEFT: *The north porch, a meeting place for townsfolk through the centuries, and where the priors transacted business.* ①

RIGHT: *The Shelley memorial by Henry Weekes, showing the poet's wife Mary Wollstonecraft (author of* Frankenstein*) mourning over her husband's drowned body.* ②

FAR RIGHT: *The beautiful great west 'Te Deum' window (1861).* ②

seen in St Michael's Loft Museum.

On the south wall of the tower are several tablets listing some of the charitable gifts to the priory church. Many other gifts are recorded in charters dating back to the 12th century. The town's most ancient charity, the Leper Hospital of St Mary Magdalen, probably built on land given by King Ethelred to Sulfric the priest in AD985, dates back at least to 1316 and was run by the monks. Though the hospital no longer exists, its charitable work continues, administered by a board of trustees.

Turn now and look down the length of the church. Gaze in awe at the sturdy Norman pillars which rise to the triforium and which supported the first roof. Cast your eye past the parish altar of the Holy Trinity and the quire screen to the top of the wonderful Jesse screen behind the high altar dedicated to Christ the Saviour. For 900 years countless millions have stood at this place, understanding the psalmist who said 'Be still, and know that I am God'.

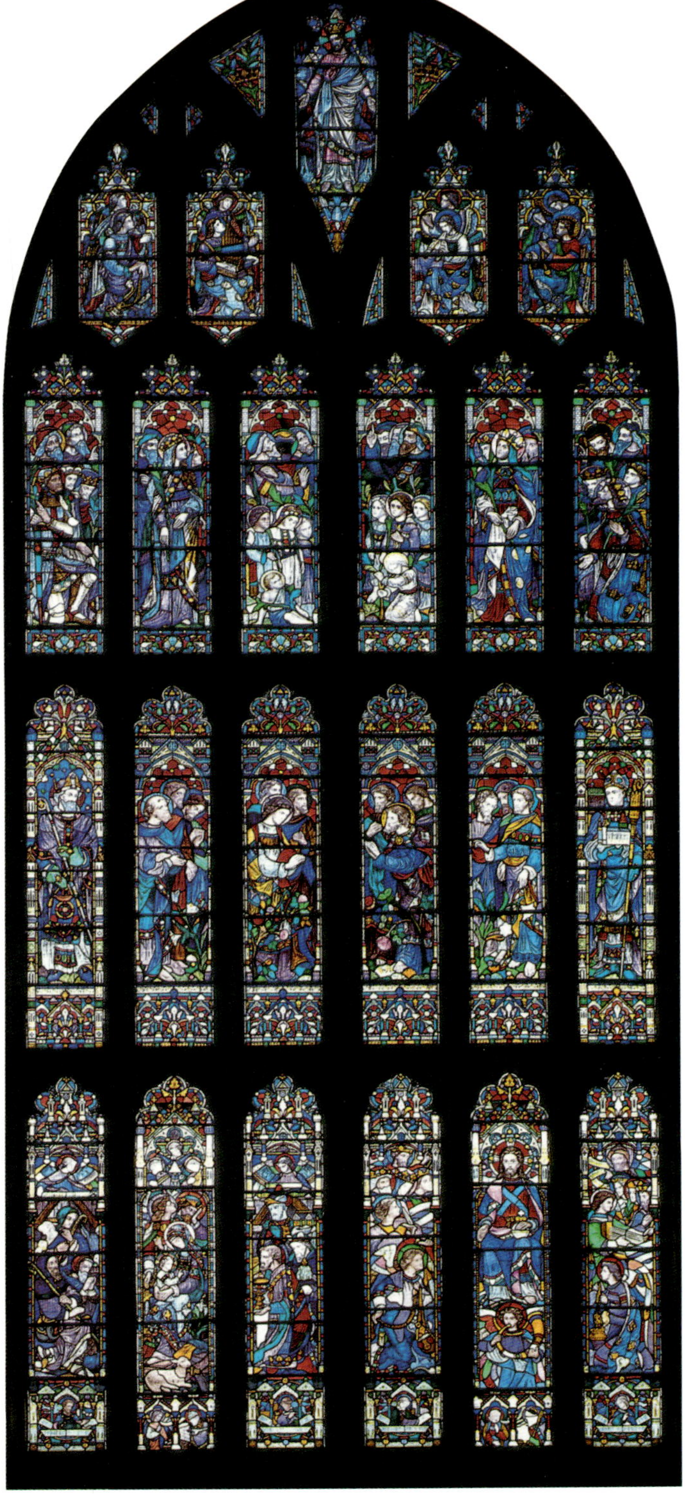

— 7 —

The Nave

The nave, with its massive pillars reminiscent of those in William I's Abbaye aux Hommes in Caen, was completed in 1150. It is considered to be one of the finest in England. Worthy of note are the regular geometrical patterns of the carving cut with a hatchet in the spandrels above the main round arches. The upper, smaller arches form the triforium, a name originally applied to the Norman triple openings at Canterbury rather than the two seen here. The central column of the south-eastern arch was removed to accommodate a pew later used by the Shelley family. The original roof spanned the nave from the corbels above the triforium. When in 1290 the clerestory was added, the roof was raised to its present height. Its massive timbers, of which the Miraculous Beam was one, lie high above the present wood and plaster vaulting put up in 1819. Many of the old roof timbers, which mostly date from 1350, are beautifully painted with flowers, dragons, angels and St George.

Frequent changes have been made to the nave over the centuries. The original stone altar stood further forward but was removed about 1540. The present altar was brought forward of the choir stalls in 1973. Originally there was no seating in the nave for the populace, who probably used the church as a meeting place as often as for worship. However as in many churches, a low stone bench runs the length of both side aisle walls for use by the infirm, giving rise to the saying 'the weakest go to the wall'.

In the south-west corner is the War Memorial Chapel which is open for private prayer. Here are housed the British Legion standards and Books of Remembrance to those who fell in two world wars and subsequent conflicts. The modern crucifix endeavours to express the pain of sacrifice. 'Greater love hath no man than this, that he lay down his life for his friend.'

The south nave aisle, over 75m (246 ft) long, gives a dramatic view down to the Draper Chantry. Note the many small carved heads either side of the south windows and elsewhere; probably contemporary representations of priests and workmen. The rounded blind arches on the south wall back onto where stood the cloister and conventual buildings which were reached by the Canons' Door through these arches. The large Prior's Door now leads to a new cloister which will contain a series of stained-glass windows depicting the historical links between the priory church and the town. Beyond the finely carved quire screen at the crossing lies the great quire, spectacularly lit by huge windows.

RIGHT: The nave looking east, with its Norman arches and fluted columns rising to the corbels, which supported the original roof. Above is the clerestory ('clear storey', since it gives light to the main body of the church).

BELOW: The central act of worship at Harvest Festival. ④

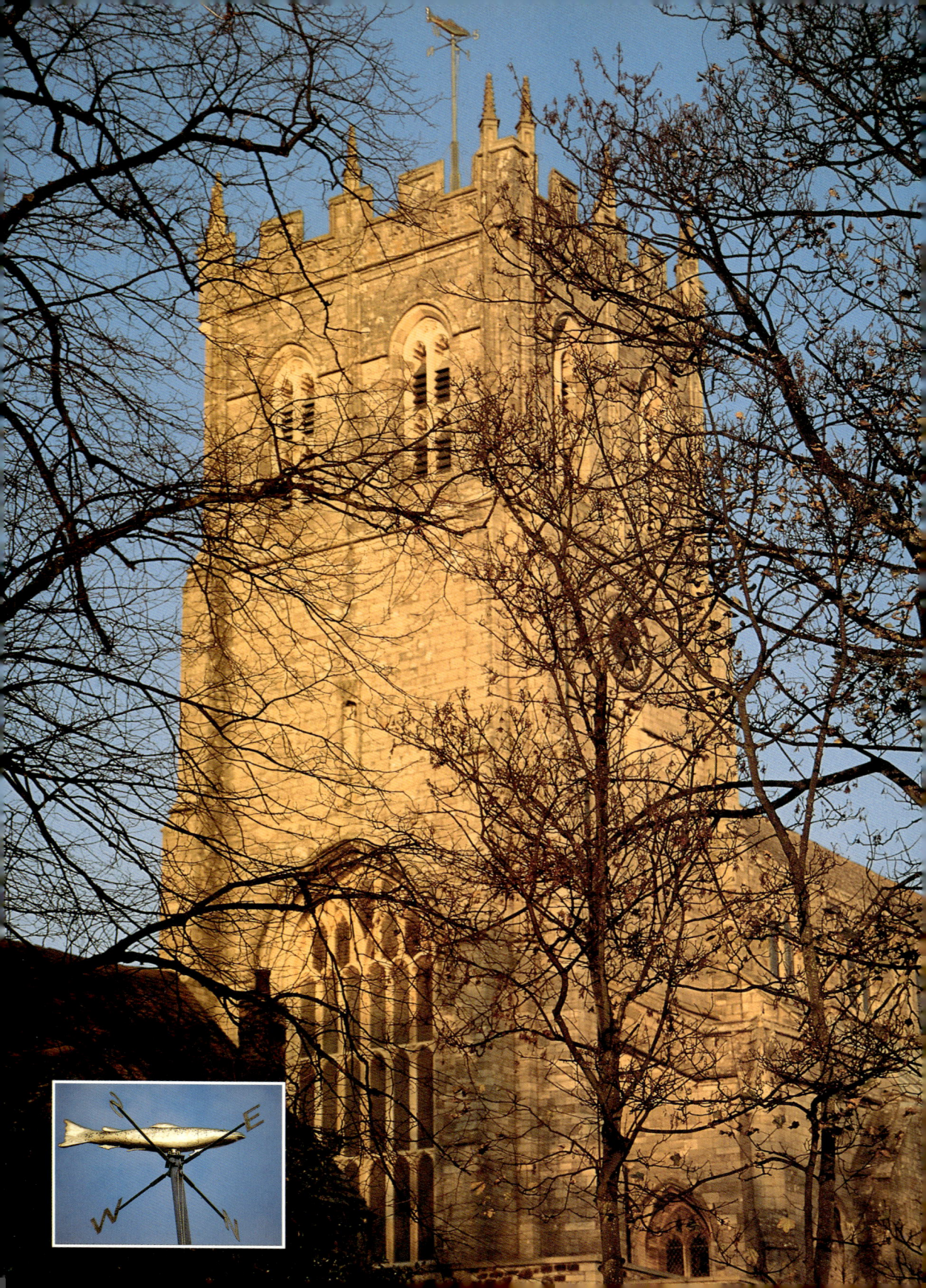

The Transepts, Crossing and Crypt

Beneath the transepts lie two of the original Saxon crypts. The north crypt, which can be visited, is apsed and has windows onto the churchyard at ground level.

In the south transept is a medieval Ascension tablet, probably from the original Lady Chapel reredos. Note the imprint of Our Lord's feet in the central stone, from which he has just ascended. There are 12 Apostles, including Matthias (see Acts 2:26). In the gallery above is the 1788 Alexander Cumming organ, rebuilt by Father Willis the elder in 1865. This now obscures a beautiful Tudor window.

Part of the 1350 roof can be seen above the crossing, where stand the massive clustered Norman columns that once supported the original tower and spire.

The beautiful quire screen, brought from elsewhere in about 1320, was installed to separate the nave, or parish church, from the quire, or monks' church. Originally it would have supported the rood loft until its destruction, along with the statues, at the time of the Reformation. The lower part is largely original and contains many delightful carvings. Look for a variety of little animals appearing just above eye level — were they from the Ark? Did the sculptor carve his own face, or was it the master mason? There are carvings of foliage on the pedestals; oak, ash, hazel and vine all found locally, and the fruits: acorns — even an empty cup — and bunches of grapes.

The inner wall of the north transept was built out with reversed stone from the destroyed conventual buildings, much of it carved. A door in the corner leads to a Saxon crypt. The floor contains some early encaustic tiles, one of which shows the arms of Eleanor of Castile, one-time owner of the Borough and wife of Edward I. The oak altar, carved by the Victorian artist Augustus Pugin, is an exceptionally fine example of his work.

LEFT: The apostles' pillar in the Montacute Chantry, showing the two-faced Judas on the left of the lower row. ⑥

ABOVE: A human face — a caricature or a portrait, and who was he? — on the 14th-century quire screen. ⑦

LEFT: The tower lit by winter sun. Inset: The weather vane (1966) above the tower, showing the famous Christchurch salmon. The fish is also an ancient Christian symbol.

RIGHT: The apsed Saxon crypt (c.AD700) beneath the north transept. ⑥

The South Aisles

BELOW: *The south quire aisle looking east towards the Draper Chantry, with the Harys Chantry on the left.* ⑰

The iron gates given by the Christchurch British Legion separate the nave from the monks' area. (The corresponding pair in the north quire aisle were the gift of the Christchurch Inner Wheel Club.) The architecture here is Perpendicular and contrasts with that of the Norman nave.

The inscription along the top of the Harys Chantry reads 'The Lord King of Blis have mercy on him (who) let make this which was Robert Harys AD1525'. A shield in the lower panel depicting a hare with 'R', and 'YS', is a play on his name called a rebus. He was one of the canons appointed to be vicar of Shroton

heathen parts' acting as a suffragan to Winchester) in 1532, Draper was forced to surrender the priory with its gold and silver plate and its annual income (£539 3s 6$^{1}/_{2}$d) to Henry VIII in 1539. However, he was granted a huge pension, £133 6s 8d (the sub-prior received only £10), and lived in Somerford manor 'a very comfortable person'. A carving above the chantry door shows the priory church with a central tower and spire and the initials J.D. The earliest of several similar carvings, dated about 1425, is carved in the stone frieze near the Salisbury Chantry. Tomb slabs of several other priors lie nearby.

(now Iwerne Courtney) in Dorset.

The door to the left leads to the largest crypt, beneath the high altar, which by its position was probably the crypt of the original Saxon stone church. It is now the family vault of the Earl of Malmesbury, the present lord of the manor.

At the end of the aisle is the chantry (now the priests' robing vestry) of the last Augustinian prior, John Draper. His tombstone, originally before the nave altar, was moved to its present position in 1840. Fragments of one of the slippers found inside his tomb are now in the St Michael's Loft Museum, the steps to which are through a door on the right. Elected prior in 1520, and probably consecrated Bishop of Neapolis (a see 'in

ABOVE: The south nave aisle looking west towards the War Memorial Chapel. ㉑

ABOVE RIGHT: Some of the Priory silver: two James I chalices and a George III flagon.

RIGHT: The shield above the Draper Chantry door, showing the initials J.D. and the Priory as it might have originally looked with a central tower and spire, before they fell in c.1420. ⑮

The Lady Chapel

The Lady Chapel, begun about 1390, is Perpendicular in style, but the glass in the east window is mid-19th century. The recently restored reredos dating from 1450 was originally decorated with bright paint and gold leaf, traces of which still remain. All the niches would have contained statues. Flanking the 3.3m (11 ft) Purbeck marble altar are the tombs of Sir Thomas West and his mother Lady Alice. He was Constable of Christchurch Castle, and dying in 1406 wished to be buried 'in the new chapel recently built at the Minster'. The modern altar rails were the gift of the Apprentices at the Military Engineering Experimental Establishment situated in the 18th-century Preventive Officers' barracks in Barrack Road, where Sir Donald Bailey developed his famous bridge in World War II. The altar rail kneelers were embroidered as part of the 900th anniversary celebrations in 1994 and depict some of the history of the priory. The beautiful lanterns at the foot of the vaulting link the Virgin Mary and medieval musical instruments in accordance with pre-Reformation rites: 'Mary is taken up into heaven; the angels rejoice'.

The flags are those of the Loyal Christchurch Volunteers, raised in 1793 to defend the coast against Napoleon (like the Home Guard of World War II). The flags contain only the crosses of St George and St Andrew since they pre-date the Union with Ireland of 1801. The Stars and Stripes was the flag of the United States forces stationed here in the 1940s. It has only 48 stars, denoting the number of American states at that time.

Backing onto the great quire screen is the memorial to Gustavus Brander, a generous benefactor. He installed the first organ in 1788 at a cost of £500, and established the annual 'Coach and Horses Sunday' sermon to commemorate his deliverance from drowning when his coach plunged into the Thames. Below it is a pewter panel of the Carpenter working on the Miraculous Beam, made in the first Arts and Crafts festival held in 1973. The end of the Beam can be seen projecting high up on the south side. It is placed there out of reach to prevent its further damage at the hands of pilgrims who over the centuries had cut slivers of timber from it to keep as holy relics. On the floor stands a 17th-century carved chest, long in use here. Its spring catch locks automatically when the lid is closed.

ABOVE: A bladder pipe player on one of the lanterns near the Lady Chapel. This droneless bagpipe was made of a sheepskin, with the blowpipe inserted in the neck, and the chanter in the forelegs. ⑭

RIGHT: The Lady Chapel. The Victorian stained glass depicts 15 episodes in the life of Our Lady. The central section shows the Nativity, the Crucifixion and Resurrection. ⑬

RIGHT: Two of the 1994 kneelers designed and embroidered by parishioners, showing monastic life and the links between church and town. ⑬

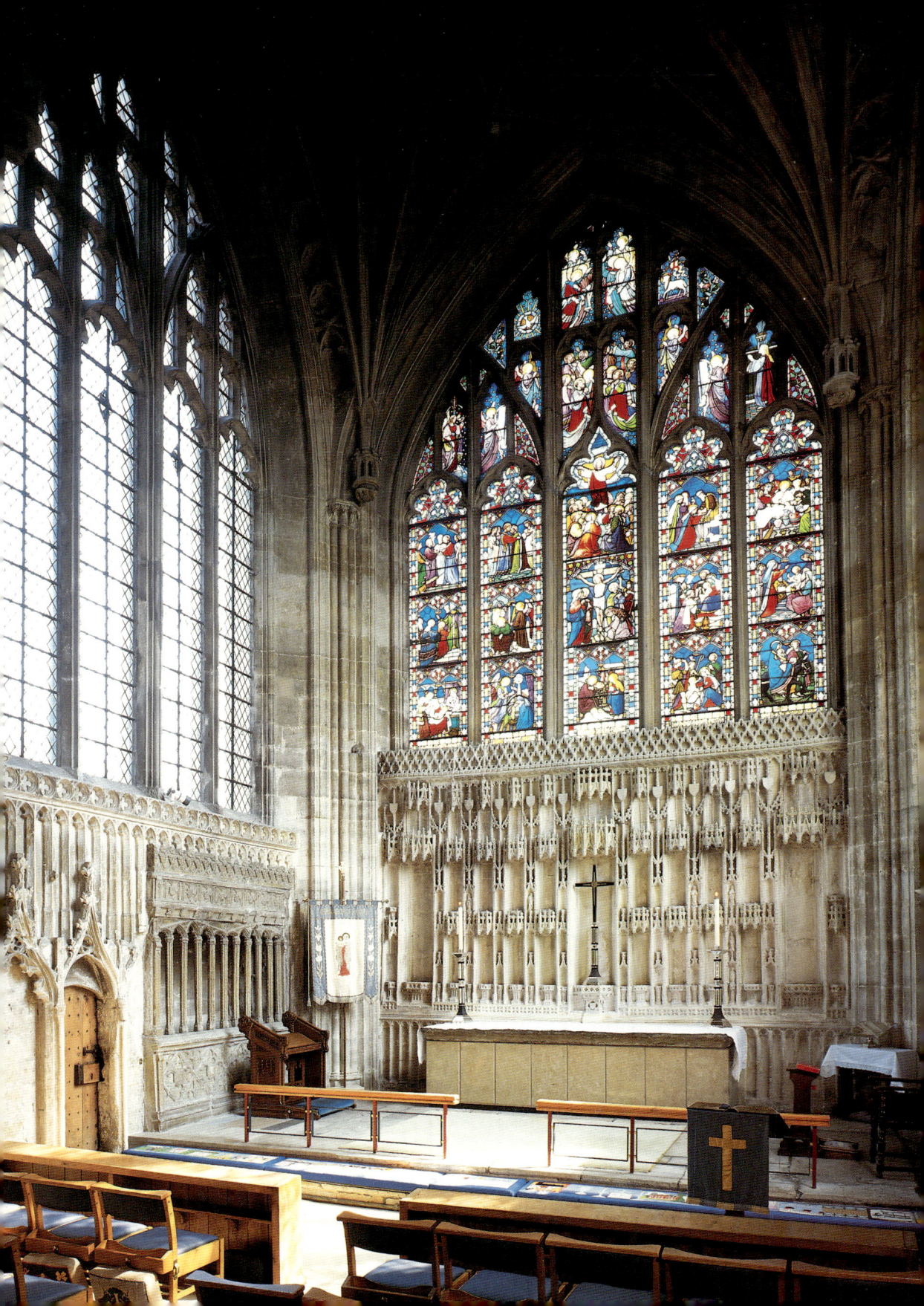

The North Quire Aisle

The tomb of Sir John (d.1449) and Lady Chidiock (d.1461) was originally below the great window in the north transept, but in 1791 it was moved to its present position beside a door leading to 'paradise', or the churchyard. His armour and her dress are late-15th-century style and he wears the double 'SS' chain of the Lancastrians.

The alabaster figures have been much defaced over the centuries, since past generations believed that scrapings from them, particularly when mixed with water from the Pure Well near Stanpit, were a cure for eye ailments.

The exquisite Caen stone design of the Salisbury Chantry is attributed to the Florentine sculptor Pietro Torrigiano.

BELOW: *The north quire aisle with the Berkeley Chantry on the right, looking towards the Salisbury Chantry and the 15th-century Chidiock tomb.* ⑨

The chantry, built in 1529 by Margaret, Countess of Salisbury for herself and her son Reginald Pole, has long been a place of pilgrimage for the faithful, who have worn the steps away. The countess, once a favourite of Henry VIII who gave her the manor of Christchurch, was the daughter of George, Duke of Clarence (said to have drowned in a butt of malmsey wine in the Tower of London). Her husband, Sir Richard Pole, was the great-grandson of Geoffrey Chaucer. When her son, training for the priesthood in Rome, bitterly attacked the king's proposed breach with the Pope, Henry, unable to reach Pole, arraigned the 69-year-old Countess for treason, though the main reason was that she had a direct claim to the throne through her father, and as such was the last of the Plantagenets. She was executed at the Tower in 1541, and was buried in St Peter ad Vincula by the Tower. The rest of her family were similarly despatched. Under Mary Tudor, Pole became a cardinal and Archbishop of Canterbury, where he is buried; so the chantry was never used. In 1542 Henry VIII ordered his commissioners to 'deface the arms, badges and inscriptions in the Salisbury Chantry', which included the ceiling roundels. Fortunately the beautiful fan vaulting and much of the fine carving including Yorkist roses and the 'planta a genista' of the Plantagenets was left untouched.

Though the origin of the Berkeley Chantry is obscure, it was probably built by William Berkeley for his parents, who around 1486 were indirectly connected with Berkeley Castle, Gloucestershire. Of particular interest are the original paintings on the walls and ceiling which show the separate red and white roses of the Houses of Lancaster and York. Was the builder perhaps hedging his bets during the Wars of the Roses?

Nearby stands a large model of the priory as it now is, enabling the visitor to see the general proportions of the church. It also houses a recording of the bells. The three painted panels nearby, dated 1702, depict the Ten Commandments, and Moses and Aaron.

ABOVE: The beautifully intricate carving on the fan vaulting of the Salisbury Chantry deserves detailed examination. Even with its defaced bosses, its richness and splendour are hard to equal. ⑩

LEFT: Victorian stained glass from a window in the north aisle. ③

The Great Quire

LEFT: An angel from the quire, holding a shield bearing imprints of the five wounds of Christ. ⑫

OPPOSITE PAGE: The great quire looking east. The 'monks' church' is dominated by the 1360 Jesse screen. Statues, which would have been painted, originally filled the now empty niches. ⑫

RIGHT: The central 'Epiphany' panel from the Jesse screen. ⑫

The beautiful reredos (c.1360) from the earlier quire survived the collapse of the central tower. When the present great quire was rebuilt about 1500 in late Perpendicular style with its huge clear glass windows, the 'Jesse Screen', as it is known, could be seen in all its magnificence. This is perhaps the crowning glory of the priory church, being among the finest in England and very little restored.

The lower figures show the Old Testament ancestry of Jesus, with Jesse flanked by David and Solomon. The 'Epiphany' panel above depicts the whole Christmas story. Taken together, they marvellously describe in stone the Christian doctrine of Christ the Saviour. This is the focal point of the monastic church. Above the reredos is the 1967 Hans Feibusch mural of the Ascension, which completes the Christian message.

The roof bosses, mostly depicting Christian symbols, and the lanterns portraying the stages of Christ's Passion contain much of the original colouring.

The misericords, tip-up seats of varying sizes on which monks could rest during their long Offices, were mostly the gift of Prior William Eyre in 1515. One, probably the oldest in England, is dated 1210. All, like the pew and stall ends, are beautifully and amusingly carved, providing cynical comment on contemporary life. Look for a salmon, Richard III and a goose seizing a jester's food. The dossiers depict many 16th-century political figures.

ABOVE: One of the oldest misericords in Britain – dated 1220. ⑫

BELOW: Detail from an elbow-rest: a cowled fox, representing a wandering friar, preaches to a flock of geese, while a cockerel on a stool acts as his clerk. ⑫

St Michael's Loft Museum

ABOVE: St Michael's Loft offers fine views north across the town and rivers to St Catherine's Hill, and south across the harbour to Hengistbury Head and the Isle of Wight. From the windows warnings were flashed to smugglers to warn them of the approach of the excise men. ⑯

Above the Lady Chapel, and reached by a spiral staircase of 75 steps, is St Michael's Loft, a large room over 17m (56 ft) long, with a fine oak ceiling. Although now a museum of the priory's history, it has twice been a school. Originally it was likely to have been a chapel of instruction for Augustinian novices, for it contains the remains of a large altar and a finely decorated piscina at the east end.

There was a school elsewhere within the priory as early as 1140. That the standard was high may be assumed from Prior Draper's plea to Henry VIII that the school 'where Divinity and Grammar are taught' be allowed to continue. It was to no avail for, with the rest of the monastery, the school was closed in 1539. But in 1662 a grammar school was established in St Michael's Loft and continued there until 1869, when the present Priory Church School was opened in Wick Lane.

LEFT: A stained-glass roundel of the ancient conventual seal taken from a document of c.1260. ⑨

RIGHT: A roundel of the ancient town seal found on several parchments. ⑨